# SUE HUBBARD

# Everything Begins with the Skin

**ENITHARMON PRESS LONDON**
**1994**

First published in 1994
by the Enitharmon Press
36 St George's Avenue
London N7 0HD

Distributed in Europe
by Password (Books) Ltd.
23 New Mount Street
Manchester, M4 4DE

Distributed in the USA
by Dufour Editions Inc.
PO Box 449, Chester Springs
Pennsylvania 19425

ISBN 1 870612 49 3

Set in 10pt Walbaum by Bryan Williamson, Frome,
and printed by
The Cromwell Press, Broughton Gifford, Wiltshire

For Ben, Luke and Megan

'Nothing but a moment of the past? Much more perhaps; something which being common to the past and the present, is more essential than both'.

Proust, *Remembrance of Things Past*

# ACKNOWLEDGEMENTS

Acknowledgements are due to the editors of the following publications in which some of these poems, in some version first appeared: *Encounter, Acumen, Ambit, Iron, Resurgence, Writing Women, Spokes, Sheffield Thursday, The Green Book* and *The Green Book Anthology, And Not Otherwise* (Poetry Business Competition 1990), *Greek Gifts* (Poetry Business Competition 1991), *In the Gold of Flesh* (Women's Press), *Klaonica: Poems for Bosnia* (Bloodaxe) and *The Blue Nose Anthology*.

'Bottling Apples' was a runner up in the Bridport Literature Festival 1988.

'Letter' was a runner up in the Poetry Business Competition 1990 and 'Secret Places' in the Poetry Business Competition 1991.

'The Convalescent', 'The Cupboard' and 'Experiment with an Air Pump' were all prize winners in the Lancaster Literature Festival 1993.

'Miss Isabella McLutchin' won fourth prize in the Peterloo Poetry Competition 1994.

The author would like to thank all those friends who gave her support and encouragement, particularly Marianne Lewin for her enduring presence and Martyn Crucefix and Mimi Khalvati for their invaluable and generous editorial contributions.

The Enitharmon Press gratefully acknowledges a grant from the London Arts Board towards the production costs of this volume.

Front cover: Eileen Cooper's *Carefully* (charcoal on paper, 125 cm x 81 cm, 1993) is reproduced by courtesy of Jason & Rhodes Gallery, London, and by kind permission of the artist.

# Contents

# PART I

## Obsession

It was a long summer
and I believed in beginnings.
Father, creator of plumbline
and saw, inventor of glue and axe,

the first to measure
the wind's drift in a web of sail,
you had made your mark:
The Labyrinth, its corridors
convoluted as thought.

But I needed visions
and possibilities, at night
dreaming, became birdman,
albatross, from my high window
heard whale song and freedom beckon.

A charcoal fire, the scent
of honeycomb heavy among the pines,
snowy down and feathers sticking
to my thumbs, I pressed

the old cockerel's hackles
into warm wax, worked like a dog
parched in the Cretan dust
while you made calculations:
rhumb, azimuth, the line of collimation.

All night I lay awake
mindful of your stern warnings:
the sea's damp spray
the searing heat of the sun.

But how could I have guessed
it would be like my first loving,
slip-stream of wind electric
as desire through pinion and plumage
the spin and roll the soar and rise
of it and I
transcendent
against a dawning disk of bronze.

Then the slow falling
the dispersion of crest and quill,
the tug and ooze of brine-soaked wings
and salt bubbles breaking
and breaking across my tongue.

## Assimilation

I never knew whether to say Amen.
In the vaulted hall silent girls dipped
rosy profiles into dust-freckled sunlight

while I stood dumb-lipped trapped by
the trinity of longing, fear, propriety,
the word stillborn in my throat.

Alone at thirteen in shadows of Dresden
blue, I bore the guilt of history, somehow
felt the weight of censure for what they'd done.

Head bowed consulting the diamond perforations on
regulation shoes, burnt ashes branded my tongue
with the double stigmata: unbeliever, hypocrite.

I did not know where I'd come from but guessed
at their journey through the snowflecked storms
of some Lithuanian December night

creeping through purple larch and spruce to flee
the zealous pogroms and their indignant Slavic rage.
Yet I've never tasted the sweet wine of Kiddush.

Beyond the stained-glass windows and the Annunciation
English playing fields stretched printed with
tramlines, the watermarks of fair play.

In the back of the cupboard in my father's study
a tarnished silver samovar lay in waiting for
tall glasses, lemon and a scoop of Russian tea.

## Secret Places

On the landing
behind the lip of wall above the stairs
I sat for hours after homework and an early tea,
after the goodnight peck when you thought me
safely tucked away in bed
lost in some jungle dream listening
to your after-dinner games of grating
the nerves' edge along the gut of a heart string.

Small buttocks bare against the freezing floor
knees hugged tight under sprigs
of forget-me-not blue,
counting particles of fluff
along the carpet's rim,
world's edge
where silver fish roamed free,
wide as a Pacific shore, my conched ear
cupped to the wall's thickness, I traced
the flaking plaster like the map to an uncharted land.

Years stretch between us now like old elastic
worn slack with too much strain, images distort,
are recreated, rearranged more safely, yet still
I can feel the bite of the icy wind in the sail,
as I set out onto that midnight sea,

to lead me from that cold place –
behind the lip of wall above the stairs
where my thumb picked at plaster flakes and the water
gurgling in radiators like the pulse of the house
sang through my head – to that forbidden adult zone,
that crimson core, dark as the places
in my body for which I had no name.

## Gloves

I remember them, fine black suede,
elegant to the elbows, elongated
as a swan's neck. A fringe
of tiny pearl buttons
revealed the vulnerable curve
of wrist, its delicate tracery of blue.

I try to imagine when she might
have worn them, picture white arms
poured like cream into the blackness,
wrapped in the couture folds of her
*New Look*, the bare curve of her shoulder,
the crimson bow of her lips.

I can still smell her dressing table
where she kept them, the stale sweetness,
the pots of waxy rouge, the perfumed chiffon.
When she was out, I hid between its skirted
legs, knees clasped in a ball, my eyes
screwed tight to make the world disappear.

## Home Movies

You show us mottled ciné films
of childhood: unreal days of honeyed
sunlight, the floral hammock
under the willow,

the salmon gladioli and the purple phlox
in bloom, our small pink bodies
glistening with droplets
from the garden spray. My sister

thin as a skinned rabbit in frilled
white bonnet, me waving,
trying to catch your eye,
wanting to play the star.

You reminisce, embellish, talk
of watching your life go by.
It is hard to see you so innocent,
so unaware, younger than I am now.

You wear your youth like a new
frock, unconvincingly. Picnics unfurl,
friends gather for drinks on the lawn
we play cricket by the sea.

When you were a child
my daughter asks,
when you were a child
and looked just like me,

so that if you and I had been
the same age then people might
have taken us for twins, when you
were a child, why was it always summer?

And in the curtained darkness,
I am forced to grapple
with the half forgotten truth,
like a censor's air-brushed man,
the facts cut out.

## The Painter's Family

*after de Chirico*

She is edgy today
her nerves all jangled
synapses stretched taut as hamstrings.

The baby's mouth opens again
a grey mollusc, the blue bruise
of colic staining its lips.

The cracks are showing.
She is becoming as crazed as the glaze
on her grandmother's plates.

She cannot carry on like this.
Her lap is too shallow, her arms
not long enough to hoop up the excess.

For he is busy. He has work to do
renewing the chipped mortar
in a wall of angles and silence.

Mute and deaf they have bound
themselves with winding sheets, filleted
down to white bone old fleshless words.

Now she must stuff the gaps, smooth
the polyfilla'd crevices in her face.
Vinegar and brown paper will no longer do.

In the orange evening dusk
she cannot open her crammed mouth
must drown her thin cries, the dim bleatings.

## Slow Slow Quick Quick Slow

Saturday mornings. The scout hall
and the boys awkward along the wall
beneath Be Prepared.
Us in white socks huddled like sheep.
My mother at Sainsbury's in the bacon queue
where girls in net turbans
slip-slapped butter on marble slabs.

Janet leading we shuffled through
the Quick Step, the Cha Cha Cha.
Miss Paddy Hackett's seamed 15 denier
legs in toeless golden shoes
clip-clopping the beat.

Then: You be the man as she clasped
me, slow, slow, quick, quick, slow
close to her cable-stitch
my eyes fixed on the Green Fern
creased under her plucked
and pencilled brow, her lipsticked teeth.

Romance? Chance would have been.
I longed for Barry, home
for the holidays in cavalry twills,
but it was always Cheryl
with the Pepsodent smile. In the Ladies
I backcombed my hair pretending
I didn't care. On the way home
in our outdoor shoes Janet and I did
*Are You Lonesome Tonight* in harmony.

## Squadron

Rowed like musical notes,
their optimism gleaming as bright
as their braid and buttons,
they sit matey and smiling
all jolly good chaps, with Jock,
the mascot dog in front,
along the fuselage. My father
– before he had that name –
and his squadron.

I remember as a child, I used to curl
in secret with the big black book,
a little guilty to be spying
on the play before my part was written in.

The jaunty uniforms, cocked hats
the stripes and wings, the honeymoon
round Cornwall in a Model T
with coupons collected in a topper
at the wedding feast, all excluded me.

Yet it was the squadron that remained –
like grey moths pinned to the dusty page –
for only three came back, my father said

and with a childish shock, I saw
their young lives cut off,
the marriages never made, the babies
never bounced with pride
on their father's knee and felt
a sudden creeping fear, an uneasy frailty.

## Licking the Dew off Roses

*(for Laurie Lee and his daughter Jessy)*

When she woke, at six in the morning,
gurgling, he'd creep silent from his
warm bed to lay her gently on a shawl.

Always the same way round they'd walk
the garden, listening to the peonies
and poppies open. He had never heard them

stretch and squeak until he walked
with her safe in his arms, laughing,
as she leaned to lick the dew off roses.

Even now she remembers frosty mornings
wrapped in a rough blanket, his flat vowels
curling in a tobacco tang, the stubble of his chin.

Oh why did you never walk with me, Daddy,
safe in your arms, under a waxing moon,
so I too could lick the dew off roses?

## Inheritance

Childhood Sundays: the dread
and the polished patina of oak
with crimson claret, the snowy
linen in initialled silver rings
and hexagrams of cutlery on
tablemats of hunting scenes –
pink coats and fox-hounds braying
for the kill and my father skilfully
carving the strained lacunae
thin as slices of rare beef.
Days when grandma came, the air
was sharp as English mustard
– she wouldn't eat the meat,
instead brought pots of pickled
cucumber, chopped liver, balls
of *gefilte* fish in waxy paper-bags
which made my mother sigh.
'It's not kosher' grandma said
when I asked *why*? unlocking
clouded memories, three generations'
climb from East End tenement
to this wooded Surrey Hill.
This was a house of tea cups,
of cupboards layered with shelves
of my father's crisp starched shirts,
of rose beds and clipped lawns,
where I learnt to stitch on
that elastic tennis-club smile
to cover the slow dawning
that I was a Jew.

## Panama Hat

The red weal under my chin
is what I remember –
sharp elastic slicing
into puppy flesh – battered summer
straw with a brown moiré trim.
At ten, a symbol of seniority,
pulled firmly down over two
braided bunches of hair,
soon to be hated, passing
the blazered boys on the bus,
as cochineal rose
the length of my throat.

Later I smashed in the crown.
On wet afternoons hid
in the art room while they picked
teams for games, from the terror
of being left till last,
savouring the smell of turpentine,
the feel of the brush.

## Letter

That familiar curving hand.
Flat and white I unfold
my mother from a single
ruled sheet, shake out
the envelope in case
I've missed her.

Our letters pass like ghosts,
thin and pale they slip
through our mail boxes.
In my dreams she comes
sweet smelling, pinched waist
in a dirndl skirt, with lint
and Savlon to make poultices
for my grazed knee. Like Gretel
I try to track the pecked crumbs
to find my way home.

                        I do not know
where to search for her. Deep
in her glass house she pricks
out seedlings, snaps yellow leaves
from last year's geraniums.

## The Convalescent

*after Gwen John*

They have changed the white cloth, soaking
out the dark stain with salt. I hardly
remember days that were different, filled
with the sweet diversions of work.
Time is measured now
in poultices and lint. Below my window
the same hens scratch the same dirt
borage and shallots bloom in the herb garden.

Hours stretch faded, formless
and I inhabit the waste lands
behind my eyelids where there is colour
for my body is white, my limbs thin
as saplings, my hair has lost its walnut sheen.
Once the bodice of this calico dress
clung tight across my apple breasts
now it hangs like a nun's blue folds.

All morning I sit by the window
read, write letters to my cousin;
outside children's voices shatter
holes in a duck-egg sky. Lilac shadows,
long and dark as a bruise, stretch
across my room, camphor and crushed
violets fill the throttled air,
on my table a pink cup and saucer of camomile tea.

From behind drawn blinds sunlight needle-
points the satin gloom. My skin is grey
as old pastry. In my wicker chair,
with the down cushion plumped to the small
of my back, I dream of the impossible sun
high over courtyard and dovecot
illuminating the frailties of small lives
baking the cracked roofs of barns.

## Bed

In this bed we first made love
and huddled in the close darkness
whispering, planned
the pattern of our future lives.

Here I bore my sons:
panting in pain
glazed eyes fixed on
pink petalled walls.

Now we lie backs turned –
trapped in our separate dreams
as I lie shivering, listening
to the banging of the chicken house door.

## Lullaby for Megan

Milk-laden, heavy with night,
mole head, velvet, blind
ferreting and sucking
at my swollen breast,
all mouth and griping hunger –
we sit watching the whitening dawn
crack like a shattered egg shell
on a sleeping world

and I wonder if one day
you too will sit,
drowsy and heavy breasted,
listening to the silent dark
and watch the damp morning
break across the hills
and have dreams of leaving?

## The Gardener

All day she battles to plant
bean poles for scarlet runners,
back curved to turn the loamy

winter earth. Wind gusts across
the valley, creates storms in
the cattle's trough, bending dock

and thistle against the dry stone wall.
Smoke billows and coils from the tall
chimney-stacks, sulphur catches

in her nostrils, rasps at the throat,
washing snaps on the line like the joints
of an old man's finger.

In her palm the crinkled beans sit
freckled, lifeless, the epiderm hard
as nail parings. With the ball of her thumb

she presses the dry shells slowly
into the wet soil. Such an act of faith
that scarlet flowers will burst

from the cold darkness. All night
it rains, rivulets of mud
furrow the dark green spinach leaves.

In her sleep she knows the poles
cannot hold, are too shallow-rooted.
At dawn she hears the snap with resignation.

## Four O'Clock

In the heat of the afternoon she lifts
a damp curl from her brow, slips
a nervous hand to her flushed neck,
absently to count the finely knotted

pearls. Beneath her armpits dark rings
form, her printed floral dress dampens,
sticks to her full thighs. Muslin curtains
billow in the heavy air, the silence

of her dark kitchen spreads like melting
butter, where the table sits ready,
neat and pretty as a new pin.
What is the point, she wonders,

knife-blade poised to cut cucumber rings
transparent as pale skin, of all this
buttered bread, these mounds of scones
in Mother's dishes, the golden gooseberry jam;

why do I disturb the cobwebbed corners?
Standing in the doorway, she waits –
bees hover in the asparagus bed –
and watches shadows lengthen across the lawn.

In a blue lipped jug, milk
separates from the cream in the warmth,
pollen falls from a vase of marigolds
dusting the white cloth yellow.

## Bee Dance

On the lip of the hive she spreads
her stained-glass wings
in a mirage of movement

stepping out her tiny tiger dance
like the songlines of ancient men
dreaming desert tracks across the bone bush.

With each quiver, each vibration
of her humming frame, she maps
in the whirring soundless tarantella,

the route; past scraggy hawthorn
and newly furrowed field, to the
old stone trough, stagnant with lichen slime.

Like some minute crazed Salome
she dances out the promise of drunken
pollen afternoons, of fleshy purple bells.

## Vermeer's Kitchen Maid

An Easter light, watery as whey, spills
from the high window, catches the rim
of her linen cap, its white gulls' wings,
the coarse cross-stitch of yellow bodice
against her apron's blue, the sleeves
rolled to elbows against curdy skin.

Already she has raked ashes, broken bread
for him from the willow basket with her big
raw hands. And in the oyster-grey of morning
while the house still sleeps, Vermeer's woman
pours warm milk from terracotta
jug to crock in silent communion.

She is mistress here,
moving with slow deliberation through
these daily tasks: her quiet meditations.
On the table beside her is spread
a Delft flagon of ale, a cloth; on the wall
a wicker creel, new polished brass.

Did he love her? Who can say?
As in the chill dawn he lifts his brush
to catch that creamy curve of brow
the shadow on her lowered lid where
sable tufts stroke, soft as her cool
fingers on fresh laundered ecru.

## Breadmaking

I wonder if they will remember that smell
on winter afternoons, the big ones
returning from school to the warm kitchen:
the foaming head that grew to the lip

of the earthen jug when we whisked
beads of yeast, fermenting
into sugar water, blood-warm to the touch?
My daughter, tiptoe on a chair

bound to the armpits in apron
sprinkled salt, rubbed fat with chubby hands
into sandcastles of speckled flour,
moustached and bearded by the brown dust.

And after, we plunged arms up to elbows
in wet dough, thumping and pulling to elastic
the heavy mound on the deal table,
slapping each portion into greased tins

to prove on the flagged-stone
floor by the fire until they rose
to a coarse-grained crust:
I wonder if they will remember that smell?

## Bottling Apples

She dreamt they were apple picking
under the gnarled apple tree.
Her children barefoot, brown as earth,
draw down the sky,
dip their fingers in its deep pool
to pluck fruit green as stars.

Later she will sort what they
have gathered in their white basins,
pare the whelk-shaped rind,
core and trim where wasps have buried
striped abdomens into the sweet flesh.

Each action careful, measured
as her sugar scoops she cuts and chops,
skims the foaming scum like skin from a wound
and into the clear jars, sealed with wax
for preservation, she carefully pours her face.

## Making Jelly

All day the juice dripped
like liquid time, fuchsia
against the white enamel rim,
clear as claret, if patient
and not hurried with a wooden spoon
disturbing the fruity sump.

Past dogroses denuded already
to hairy crimson hips, a scrub
of dock and battered aluminium
trough, over earth pock-marked with
hoof-prints that trapped wellingtons
and reached above your knees,

down into the valley's steep
throat, with plastic bags
and kitchen bowls we tumbled
to pick the last late fruit,
competing with blowflies
and the first bruising of frost.

Now that bleeding muslin seems
a life away. The slow erasure
of memory clouds like impure jelly,
the picture fading as the filming
of an ageing eye. Do you even
remember that pungent yeasty smell?

Here in this empty house these things
seep back, disturbing the silence.
Outside leaves choke the gutters
as sparrows compose themselves
on city wires against
the deep flush of a Rothko sky.

## Taboo

Here she comes again
the old hag
out and about
whining and wheedling

just one bite
she croons
just one little bite
won't hurt, peppermint pink
and sweet caramel.

Solitary beneath the bedclothes
I unwrap them, rowed
ruby red and emerald green
the gold foil glistening

and in the dark silence
of the sleeping house,
creep, dragging my guilt
like a tattered night gown

to the kitchen –
ashamed that love
has been reduced to this
the glutinous remains
jellied and pale
of children's leavings.

## The Curse

She is all woman now
daughter become sister
spindle-prick of peony
smearing her whites.

A butterfly wing of bright
crimson surprises her waking,
shyly she comes to me bringing her
ring-o'-roses, her scarlet bouquet.

We are joined in blood
by the slow pull of the moon's
waning and the small secrets
of darkened bathroom shelves.

How the past echoes. My mother's
silent mouthing of those witchcraft
words. The Curse, as she taught me
to name that first staining.

Have we forgotten those cackle
voices; conspiratorial whispers
echoing among unguents and tinctures
in white-tiled rooms?

And I who was mute, spineless
as a sea-horse, wish you brave
and beautiful. Feel your roots, deep
and damp as rusty beets smelling of earth.

## Driftwood

I found it
on the beach
in winter the day
my marriage fell apart

the wind blew from Ireland
boring into our skulls
it jutted from shingle bleached
blade-bone, honed sharp by sea

I held it close
a touchstone against
your white silence

– I want to go home I said

tucking it inside my oil skin
like an animal
protected from the cold

– a hooded eagle
head rearing in
its death throes
the sinews of the neck
taut, distended

where the grain darkens
into twists and knots
the hollow bowl forming
an empty eye:
now it sits
on the marble mant!epiece
like a work of art

## The Beach at Trouville

*after Eugène Louis Boudin, 1824-98*

The wind is up:
tossing the gritty sand
into the stamping horses' eyes.

Dogs circle and yelp
across the wide wet sands
snapping at bladderwrack

as the ribbons of her straw hat
whip in the breeze.
She stands a little apart

from the beaux and belles
of Trouville, pretty
under ruffled parasols

their satin hooped crinolines
parachuted by the salty gusts.
For soon this giggling group

will tire of 'oohs and aahs'
and leave this afternoon's blowy
*mise-en-scène* for Monsieur Henri's

fine *cognac, chocolat* or *café au lait*
and she will gather up her loneliness
and black *crêpe* skirts in handfuls above

the knee, to search the shoreline
for razor shells and tiny crabs hidden
in pools between the damp worm casts

while hissing breakers
roll and slip, spattering her wind-
burnt skin with spots of tangy spray.

## Starfish

I never wanted a daughter,
saw myself as the mother
of sons, a male tribe;
was afraid to re-discover
the girl who couldn't make
sense of it all, who stood on
the cream cusp between
daylight and dark
between cobwebbed shadows
and curdy morning
not knowing which way to turn.

I wanted boys; knotted limbs
strong as the branches of beech
that tap-tapped at my bedroom
window where I dreamt you;
boys who would travel
in a straight line away
from my need as rockets
seek stars, not reflect self
back to self – a dish of moon
cradling its swimming face
in the puddle of the hens' pen.

Then you arrived, my alike-
as-two-peas-in-a-pod daughter,
my-almost-twin, clattering down
the street in my too high
heels, bringing me
starfish on a windy beach.

Now oceans have rolled in
between us and you have set
sail for your lost father –
meetings and partings, partings
and meetings – though one day
you may turn around, back across
the dark water, and see your mother
waiting with starfish at her feet.

## Filling the Spaces

Love and need conceived them
to fill the blank space,
that moment in the bloody darkness.

Huge helmets of bone
lay snug and tiny petalled mouths
sucked sprouting fingers,
budding clusters of pink anemones.

Nine months of bliss we had,
you anchored like a boat to my belly,
rocking, rocking
in silvered amniotic oceans.

Still I hold
the memory of the moment
we first met,
separate, human
face to face,
I cried at your completeness
and the pain of knowing
this was already
the beginning of the end.

You have grown:
seedlings nurtured
by my need, reaching out
towards
the light,
the moment
of your own flowering.

And I am thrown back
as you rush careless from the house,
heads stuffed with football and friends,
to that blank space,
seeking new labels and definitions
among the dirty socks
and discarded breakfast things.

## Letter to my Son

I would write you a letter
and slip it beneath your door
like a timid lover, to ask
forgiveness for my quick tongue,
for I can no longer simply
take you in my arms and say
my anger does not belong
to you, you would grow
embarrassed, beetle-browed
and stiffly shrug me off. Nor
can I presume your love –
sit you on my knee to peel
oranges in the shadows
by a winter fire
or curl, warm limbs entwined
at the bottom of my frowsty bed
beneath a tent of sheets.

I did not see it happen,
the point of separation,
the reclamation. Now I must woo
and cajole you, a stranger,
admit my fault.

I would write you a letter
and slip it beneath your door.

## Across the City

Beyond wicker blinds
a sea of green. Not tender
as in spring, but a darkened,
mid-summer green, sage
as the coating on a stagnant pond.
The leaves on the plane tree
hiss and swirl, tidal in July wind.
So quiet here, people say,
you can't believe it's London.

Again I wake alone,
imagine those doing so
by choice or habit:
children, nuns, the very old
and in the thin grey light
of morning do not recognise
this place where dreams have shrunk
to pinheads and longing has become
as dry, etiolated, as the bathroom
geranium we all forget to water.

Forty four. Mid-way if I'm lucky
and keep up the aerobics.
I feel too young to be this old.
Loss forms the bass-note,
as little by little,
this body betrays me
and somewhere, out there,
you go on living.

My friend telephones to say
her man is too busy to see her.
He offers promises
fragile as egg shells
and all across the city
I hear the urgent wail
of women waking to become less
than their sleeping selves,
striving to find a common web
of words, to bind stone hearts,
looped tight as columbine.

For how are we to live?
We, who have tried love,
marriage, borne children,
bathed wounds, written books,
manoeuvred the mountains' craggy gaps.
What other possibilities unfurl,
as we wait in the quiet of vacant
rooms for our futures to define us?

# PART II

## The Cupboard

Her grandmother's cupboard is made
of painted cedar. She remembers
– how old was she? Five? – unpegging
stiff boards of white sheets,
bleached from the sun, folding them
into the wicker basket in the yard.
And the singed steaming of cotton
cooling on the backs of chairs.
Then up the dark stairs to pile them
neat as stone slabs. One shelf always
kept for winter blankets smelling of camphor.

She loved the doves in each corner
of the doors, a floral garland strung
from beak to beak, the swirls of
eucalyptus leaves. A garden to get lost in.

Now winter is coming.
Last night the wind blew her candle out
broken glass rattles in the panes
like ill-fitting teeth. There has been
nothing to eat for weeks. The neighbours
rumour of snipers, of convoys, they say
Hassan's lorry couldn't get through.

In the corner she watches her daughter
Jasna huddled in her brother's big coat,
poking out the bullet eyes of old potatoes
– her own mother lies under a fresh
mound of earth. And in the dim lamp-light,
as she scrapes the green skins, she knows
that there will be no more laughter
of mothers of daughters unpegging
sundried sheets in the yard.

The cold is burning their fingers,
the cold is turning their chapped
hands red. Yet still she would give
her daughter a garden to walk in
a garden of eucalyptus and doves...

From the back of the chair she quietly
takes her scarf and wraps it
around her shoulders. From the hook
in the yard she fetches the axe.

## Great Aunt Mina

Sometimes she comes to me in dreams
thin as ectoplasm, smelling
of lavender water that seems
stale as her powder-dribbled chiffon

twisting, twisting her sparse hair, she calls
out, trailing her confusion like a tattered
bridal gown down those stained Victorian halls
in a glissade of despair.

Her egg-shell mind convulsed into a near
approximation of sanity: the clamped
electric wires, the rubber bite, the fear,
cold and sharp as the clinch of steel.

I never knew her, hers was a name
whispered faint as an exhale of breath
in quietened rooms hushed with shame,
behind locked adult doors.

Now I wonder why they put her away
among pruned roses and neat clipped lawns
behind high walls that shut out the day
from the memorial gardens of the not-quite-dead.

Sometimes in passing I catch sight
in a fractured glass or butcher's shop
of a panicked face, that some might
just for a moment, think they remember.

## Beyond my Window

                    the city
flows fast as a river
buildings jut like trees
against the skyline
where frightened people cling
for shelter in their branches.

In secret rooms
girls and old men paint
their faces, bind bones
polished and white as snow,
head to neck, neck to spine,
straight-backed they travel
up and down the windy escalators
stiff with grief.

High in a dark room, the woman
waits behind her door,
shivers
wrapping the night close
about her like a shawl and listens
for the mail train going North.

## Kimono

Hanging on the hook behind the door
its batwings wilt lifeless
as paper kites in need of wind,

coiled dragons breathe fire
and pink chrysanthemums
blousy as showgirls

emblazon the flaccid scarlet silk
that other times has clung
sensuous and inviting to warm skin.

But tonight, it is too much.
I cannot play the geisha,
live up to its expectations,

it demands too much beauty.
Tonight, with candlewick
and cocoa, I shall try

to build a wall against
the silence that seeps
beneath my door.

**I dreamt I remembered what love was**

For one fraudulent moment,
with your lips on my hardening breast,
our bodies strange in the darkness
pressed close in the promise of that narrow bed –
our alien selves,
our fears,
shed momentarily,
hung up on the hook behind the door,
I dreamt I remembered what love was.

Bound together by darkness,
unfamiliar limb exploring
unfamiliar limb in
temporary tenderness,
the soft dawn rain outside
my hair tumbling like a cliché on your chest,
I dreamt I remembered what love was.

## Counterpoint

Through my window Victorian
façades of intricate red brickwork
stare at me, dumb as strangers,
lime trees stand imprisoned
in pavements, their eczemaed skin
blemished and raw.

No blood holds me here,
no soil roots me
in this accidental place,
this house contains
only a sort of present.

No drawers filled with my mother's
silk scarves, the scent of crumbling
roses, or the ivory-headed bristle
brushes embossed with my father's name.

Adrift with my children
there are no memories,
daily we throw out lines
to anchor our lives.

On my desk the feather of a buzzard,
brought by a man whose face
I've long forgotten, yet kept
for some reason, white quill in a jar –

barred and speckled, an ariel tiger,
a counterpoint to this urban living,
a talisman back to the open fields,
the wooded valley, that other wilderness.

## Chaos Theory

I heard a scientist
say the flutter of
a butterfly's wing
could cause a tornado,

that the theory of
cause and effect
has been shaken to the roots,
that we cannot reduce

hurricanes, floods, the knife edge
of a lightning flash, anger
or an accidental death
to a neat equation.

The Greeks got it right
after all it seems,
we were born from Chaos
spat out on a sea of pot luck,

Chaos who spawned mother earth,
the sky, oceans
from her clay haunches,
the ochre dust of her giant thighs.

Move one decimal point
the scientists said and our lives
run on a different course,
instead of hope there is despair

or the carrot fly blighting
a near perfect crop. In the
silent pond a thousand tadpoles spawn
beneath the shadow of the stickleback.

Like schoolboys knocking
marbles in the asphalt yard
we ricochet off
what life throws up

fall like the yarrow sticks
of a Chinese soothsayer,
straw blown in the gusting wind,
hinged on a fluke of chance.

# Experiment with an Air Pump

*after Joseph Wright of Derby, 1734-97*

That night we gathered,
the white moon peeped between the skirted clouds
flooding the high-panelled room in eerie light.
Eight of us, at the great scientist Dr Wilks's house,
a man with eyes so deep and brows so fierce,
in copper damask dressing-gown, he frightened me;
and that shock of wiry hair!

On the table such weird contraptions as I'd never seen:
an air pump made of gleaming brass, strange tubes
and liquids that gave a sulphurous glow.
I cried and hid my eyes, clasped Kitty close,
at six far braver and more curious than I.
Still I can feel the callused grip of Joshua's
hand in comfort on my thin shoulder.

Science: an experiment, he explained,
to see if the pretty bird could fill
its gasping lungs and beat its failing wings
without the magic stuff he called oxygen.
I could not bear the thud of its snowy breast,
the rattle of its brittle beak, the scratch
of tiny claws, as it circled and circled
expiring from want of air.

Such power of life and death he had
that strange alchemical man
I did not dare cry out 'stop' to save
the frightened thing.

Later, when they were finished, I asked
to hold the soft limp body, sat by
the guttering candle on the sill
and tried to close its beady current eyes
as a lick of scarlet dribbled from its beak
and felt the little bones
light as air in my warm cupped hands.

## 'I Carve to the Beat of the Heart'

*Barbara Hepworth*

From her high window
an arc of blue
almost Aegean
where white gulls circle
and mew against
a canvas of Cornish light.

Below an oasis of shadows
palms and mirroring pools
a garden
where sculptures grow like trees;

an ochre jacket, overalls stiff
with dust, still hang expectant
behind the greenhouse door
mallet, chisel, drill,
the paraphernalia of a mason's art
seem only momentarily set aside.

On her bench a block of stone
white, unhewn, waits
in perpetuity for her hands
to set free the trapped planes of light.

In the silence
her heartbeat
the punctured cry of gulls.

## Button

shade of polished sage
a button dropped from your coat
sits by my bed
green and still as a small pond
four round eyes stare back
in blank silence

you took your shaving things
but it is said
those who leave something behind
one day return

once by a lake
where we watched geese skim
and slide across the brown surface
my lips brushed your jacket
a slash of crimson maybe
still decorates the lapel

## I would as easily

                    scour
the ocean's bed, the depths
where skate and stingray
lie flattened in mottled shadows
and albino fish, blinded
by the dark, slither across
the icy floor to feed
on translucent plankton

or walk slakeless among
the dunes of Arabia –
shifting as an inland sea –
where only nomads know
the intricate criss-cross
of invisible paths that lead
to groves of tessellated pools
trickling among date palms

or step into uncharted
magnitudes of space
where quarks and electrons
expand and cool, where matter
spirals back into its own being

as traverse
the closed borders of your mind,
that unknown country.

## Rosehips

Flat and yellow
the morning rolls in
across the bleached salt pans
across the iron mud,
drab as an old blanket,
too timid to turn to day.

Beneath thinning stars
it unfolds across
brittle reeds
that rattle and moan
below the verandah
where she sits
eyes narrowed
to some far-off horizon.
The green door laps
a cat's tongue
at the gusting wind,

and in the whitening sky,
the waning moon
dims the rhythms
of her catamenial womb,
maps each wordless sigh
across the contours
of her face,
a silent cartographer.

With the side of her thumb
she bursts bitter rosehips
sucks out the tiny seeds.

## Sisters in Waiting

other women's men
her life was littered
with other women's men

second hand lovers
with thrift shop caresses
stained and yellowed from over-use

boring like woodworm into
the rich grain of her life
the dips and crevices of her tousled bed

in the darkness their bruised
wives count in whispers
each brittle second

behind their thin-lipped smiles
until the reassurance
of the lock's click

her sisters in waiting

as other nights she sits
peeling torn skin
from the half moon of fingers

like pith from an orange
circling the forbidden phone
the sickness in her stomach rising

across the room the screen
flickers with images of love
like a silver catechism

mocking her with each plastic
embrace – held between the
twin pincers of pain and pain

a fish caught on a hook
she gasps for breath

## Telephone Calls

In the spaces stretched from here
to there, across roof-top and barn

between waste-ground or gullied railway track
wires carry the shape of our aborted words

mouths purse into ovals of silence
until all we can feel is the hurt.

We have known all along since I first urged you
those six hot miles through Aegean August dust

down that pink dirt track beneath blue-
webbed pines, past farmstead and figtree

hayrick and olive to the rocky spur where
Foukas Bay lies glistening

that what you and I meant by this and that
is different. For words roll like white pebbles

across our muzzled tongues but unlike
poor Demosthenes, our stammering does not stop.

## Divinations

I write your name across the page in thick
black script. My own fits snugly underneath
– a trick I learnt at school – to slash in pairs

twinned letters, two sibling Ss,
the double Es and with the sum that's left
count he loves me, loves me not…

My world is made of signs. Magpies for sorrow
and for joy. I avoid the pavement cracks,
disregard the news of world events

for Star Signs by Patrick Walker. Add dates
and times in significant contortions. If I could
I'd read the tea leaves in my mug, lay out old

chickens' bones, hang up dry seaweed to gauge
the drift and shift of things. Like an obi-man
peeling back loose flaps of skin to see

the flesh beneath, I peer into dim tomorrows
to check if you're hidden there. I'm bored
with waiting for something to happen

trying to conjure you from this bald white
page. Don't offer me enigmas, Chinese puzzles
and conundrums simply to avoid

the pain of real communion. At night
in secret, I slip silver coins
through my fingers – a ten piece drachma

kept for luck – and in the yin and yang
of hexagrams try to decipher the future's
script to see if you could love me.

## Woman Bathing in a Stream

Some days Bathsheba or Danaë
voluptuous and bangled
on her cushioned ottoman. But this evening,
her linen chemise crumpled high
against wide hips, the loose
sleeves carelessly rolled, she paddles
the stream, simply herself, Hendrickye.

Florentine brocade, mulberry damask
from Uzbekistan, she leaves the tumbled rugs,
steps in the pool, her body warm, the smell
of him lingering still between her thighs.
His eyes absorb the creamy solid flesh,
those familiar dimpled knees. He makes
no judgement on her nakedness.

Times she has posed for him;
out of love, not an interest in his art,
just as each morning she pours his ale
chops pickled herrings, slices coarse black bread,
nights warmed his bed since Saskia died.
Nurse to small Titus, what difference,
opening her ample arms to him as well.
No matter others find him strange.

Soon dusk will turn to night, wood-smoke
and a Gouda moon hang over the gabled house.
She turns to her mirror, combs out her hair
prepares for sleep, sees other selves reflected
in her glass: the sandy freckled skin. Let him
wrap her in *chiaroscuro* if he must – grey morning
will find him seeking the warmth of her bed.

* *Saskia was Rembrandt's first wife, Titus his son*

## Miss Isabella McLutchin

She had always dreamt of this –
among the Calvinist shadows of grey Edinburgh
afternoons in anaglyptic drawing rooms –
the stripping of whalebone corsets, stepping
from those stiff, hooped skirts.

Wet childhood Sundays, after chapel,
nose pressed Eskimo to leaded window panes
watching the granite rain, she conjured swamps
and savannas where the beryl eyes of tigers
burned yellow through swaying grass.

They tried to dissuade her, of course,
but Miss Isabella McLutchin had done with
button-hooks and gloves, the arsenic powders
to whiten freckled skin, understood that
sandy complexions were not meant for love.

So she bound her unnecessary breasts,
packed a tin trunk and shipped it
to the hubbub of a foreign port, abandoned
the absurdities of sidesaddle for the feel
of leather creaking between her thighs.

Then tanned and cross-hatched from desert sun,
she slept, for coolness, with a quilt
in inner yards. In Quashgiai she bathed
in streams with the women fully clothed,
their multi-layered skirts splayed
in coloured circles like giant lily-pads.

## The Carpet Merchant

Wary as an animal she sniffs the air
enters the colour of wounds, shadows
of crushed aubergine, the cedar dark
where fretted shutters jigsaw the blazing light.

Outside the cries of saffron vendors
fade, the clatter of the bazaar
where fair-haired English teachers
flirt with traders for Turkish delight.

Elegant he sits her on soft cushions
nods to the olive boy to bring her *cayi*
and limpid apple tea, clicks his fingers
to conduct his symphony of rugs

which unroll like prayers. The knots
are looped and dropped, he explains,
for perfection belongs to Allah.
He offers her weaves of indigo,

of faded cochineal, where trellises
of butterflies symbolize the transience
of love, and corrugated arcs a nomad's
thirst for waves. He tells her this was

his father's house. How as children
they jumped naked to the sea from the carved
balcony, as he pushes to the shutter,
brushing a cool hand against her white shoulder.

## Guest-Worker

It is his home.
He knows no other.
A new language now eases
more fluently across his tongue,
erases memories of mountains,
the mullahs' sunset cry
the Cappadocian valley where
he herded his uncle's sheep
into the elbow of a rocky stream,
the terraced tobacco gardens.

And in his dreams
he rolls up his prayer mat
around his mother tongue
sheds it like excess baggage
at secret borders.
For he is seven – always seven –
crossing those ridges of snow
vertical as drying sheets
footfall on cold footfall
in his brother's tracks
the fear inside him frozen
as small fingers.
Cardboard and string.

Today he has nearly forgotten Tokat,
its narrow streets
where upper floors of timbered houses
jut like chins,
and those fine moustaches playing
backgammon in the dust
under the shadows of a backyard vine,
the click-clack of beads,
a dish of olives, a glass of *raki*
in a work-scarred hand,
the smell of rosemaried mutton
through an open window.

Now he rises at five
and in the concrete cold
methylated petals flickering
violet in the dark, boils water
for his tea on the spirit-lamp
brought from childhood,
turns up his collar
to the northern chill
as the empty subway sucks
him in, the scrawled graffiti
jeering like a premonition.
Then on the silent factory floor
with mop and broom
sweeps the leavings of fairer men.

At night he hurries home
through hostile streets
turns the TV loud, to drown
his sister's mounting fear,
the sparks of hatred
that ignite like petrol plumes
to stop his nostrils fill his ears.
The *Sieg Heil, Sieg Heils*,
shattering
like windows inside his head.

## Archangel

And he said:
in my dream
there was this black man
with his beatific face
and sweet smile,
hanging like an angel,
dangling from a rope
around his waist,
high above the crowds
at Charing Cross.

As I passed
he called down to me laughing:
– *Watch this*
*men have died falling from this height!*
At his neck,
pinned like a débutante's rose,
a brilliant pronged star
shimmering, sharp,
glistening
against his throat,
the tips like razors.

And then it happened:
the rope snapped,
the world spun,
plunging him to concrete below,
the point of the star
piercing his tongue
a crystal explosion
of silver rain
tinged with scarlet.

Slumped on the pavement
he lay –
splinters of glass decorating
the wound of his mouth,
blood, mirror, mouth:
a pink tongue
pinioned by a star.

## Blight

'...we're compressed into
this single span of opportunity
for which our gratitude should categorically be presumed'

*C. K. Williams*

and hearing his words unblocked something in her like the
cleaning of a faucet or a drain, unblocked the pain, a gush
gave her courage to call out to strip that supermarket face

that capable fixed smile, to admit to being merely human, to
nightly tears at the implacability of things, at the slow
erosion of this single span. Who asked anyway, was it Chekhov,

why we do not lead the lives that it is in us to lead? And she
does not know whether she cries for herself or for the white-
faced boy with the blue shaven head begging wrapped in a

tattered blanket on the steps of the tube, for her need and his
have melded into a laser point of unity at this slow seepage
of time, and she cries because she knows each day on waking

she is older, the callous indifference of ageing, its crumples
and creases, etched through the night deeper on her paper
    cheek
and at the loss of illusion and this searing emptiness,

the illusion that the odour of skin, a tongue tip full in the
mouth, the twining and intertwining of limb of muscle of heart
in the razor darkness can bandage this wound this sepsis

and she knows that his youth is being eaten, being corroded
as the constant drip of rain rusts a faulty gutter, his one his
only blooming spoiled like a frosted apple crop

by this daily devaluation and her heart goes out
impotent, guilty, wanting to hold, wanting to salvage
the neglected hungry child within them both

68

## Checks and Balances

*for Luke*

I

Today I returned to my parents' house.
Not where they live now,
but where I grew up as a child.
Nothing is different, yet nothing
the same. I nearly missed the lane,
the road widened, the grassy verges gone.
I cannot be certain what I came
to reclaim, what shadowy memories.

But they have cut down the wisteria
(I had almost forgotten its purple
udders hanging outside the window)
neglected the rose beds,
the crazy-paved terrace
with the fish pond my father netted over
so we didn't fall in,
chopped down the weeping willow.

Only the japonica, preceding
the bitter quince, flaunts
raspberry flowers and my brother's broken
tree-house still sits wedged
in the high fork of the copper beech.
The orchard seems to have been sold.

And from somewhere across the unkempt lawn
I can hear the rise and fall of *Swan Lake*
crackling on a wind-up gramophone
as I and Caroline
tutued and netted, practise our pirouettes.

Now on the sweet-chestnut that was always
'home', so wide-girthed five of us,
finger-tip to stretched finger-tip
could only just encircle it,
I sit hugging the past as the tears
come, trying to find words to unlock,
to name this longing as I re-live

those tense mornings, my mother busy
in the kitchen, my father picketted
behind *The Times*, his soft shaved
cheek perfumed and tilted for my kiss
and I grieve, I grieve that we can't
do it all again, that it cannot be mended.


II
And that morning as the thin spring sun
poured through the hospital window silvering
the mercury stirrups, the shining speculum

and forceps rowed in sterile surgical precision
and the iceberg tiles of the labour room,
we came, just for a moment, close to a sort

of perfection, your father tender (the only time
I remember, the only time that has stayed locked
in my memory, buried deep as a hidden seam of coal

in the compressed earth, as if I could not give it up
as if I could not finally surrender it, having
to believe that just for a moment love was possible)

damping my cracked lips with a moist sponge.
You arrived through the pain from your own country
black hair spiked as a sea urchin's spines

your left ear tightly furled like the inner white
leaf of the cabbage I tried to grow in the garden
and a blemish dark as ripe strawberries staining

the span of your toes – your own tiny human imperfections.
And now I watch helpless, culpable, as your
adolescent anger bubbles and hisses like some

steaming Nordic geyser, your anger that I have
failed you as they in their turn failed me, that your
father's offering soured to acid, that I could not

my dear son, even out of love, make it perfect.

## Feet of Clay

Beside his, her small foot
looked absurd; square and squat
like a bloated child

toes chiselled, stubbed,
the neat red ends
a caricature of a foot

his thin, reptilian
the joints all gnarled
– kinetic toes – he said

so foot by foot in the firelight
they stood looking at them like
two separate people with nothing to say.

## Eating Pomegranates

With the curve of your thumb-nail,
you tore it in half,
pierced the tough skin
picked out the glistening
shiny seeds that bled
their red sweetness
onto the white plate.

And in the space left between
words, where adult meanings lurk
we sat at midnight, refugees
from the city's thrum and shift
filling our mouths like children
sharing sweets, with handfuls
of translucent crimson beads.

'When I was a kid', you said
'I used to eat them with a pin'.

In that cold room, wrapped safe
in our separate loneliness
you took my hand in yours,
placed sticky palm to
sticky palm until they stuck

then quickly pulled away,
as if such an act might bind
beyond mere childish playfulness.

Then you gave me a cloth
and we wiped the juice away.

## Nude with Blue Cushion

*Jeanne Hebuterne, Modigliani's mistress, committed
suicide on his death, while nine months pregnant, by
throwing herself from a window*

They deepen, satiated with desire
like the filming of trout pools
by the clouding of the sun, her sloe-black
burnt-black almond eyes.

Everything begins with the skin:
soft flesh gleaming in the knowledge
of its own perfection, recalling the recent
pleasure of his hand, the current pull of the brush.

Here she is all present; her
hip, navel, thigh utterly surrendered
to the iridescence of madder hues,
the fullness of his love.

Elongated as a languid cat
she lies; a crooked arm angling her head
against the little cushion of faded blue
reveals its damp pit of tangled hair.

Softened by hashish and hunger
she does not now concern herself with *sous*
or grey morning's marketing of bread.
Jeanne maybe? Her future as yet unwritten:

backwards, nine months with child,
through that high window.
For chaos and sweet death tonight lie drugged
with a flush of carmine, of Venetian red.

## Voyage

Florida. A holiday he said.
He's seeing someone else...
November rain beats against
her window as he soars
silver-winged over eiderdown clouds

to sundrenched beaches
where swivel-stick palms shelter
lovers in their shade and
neat boulevards seduce
nightly with frissons of neon.

And in the lemon lamplight
of her room, towelling dry her hair
her showered skin gleaming for no
particular touch or reason, she
remembers another journey

across a deep lake, the rowlocks
of their clinkered skiff creaking
in the dark, her trusting his helmsman's
hands to guide them safe across
the open water until the sudden eddy –

the split of plank from plank –
and him dipping the bladed oar
pulling against the tide to turn
towards the distant headland
leaving her drowning, nearly drowning.

## A Half Open Door

                                    into another room
and in an ashtray on an unseen table
a cigarette uncoils itself, exhales
in perfect rings into the thick night air.
Beside a bowl of oranges, empty glasses
leave their marks like the areola of trees.
Across a chair, a jacket,
draped like an abandoned dream,
and in a mirror that I cannot see
the reflection of a face I'll never know –
hidden lives, myriad as the littered stars
of lilac blooms or a thousand grains of sand.
There are other realities beyond this waking,
where the thin May rain drips outside the window.
Worlds within worlds, holding their arcane secrets
like a box of Chinese tricks or a map
of a map of the place that I seek.
Do you remember as a child, snug in the kitchen,
that picture on the cereal box of a mother
sitting at breakfast with her smiling brood,
spick and span in their warm kitchen beside
a cereal box where a mother sits at breakfast
with her children contemplating infinity?
Air rattles in the radiators,
the world still sleeps, only the pain
of the successful is justified, others
must sob unheard into damp night pillows.
I have become careless, have dropped
and scattered years, minutes, seconds
like used bus tickets, made balls
of fluff with discarded days in
the pocket lining of some forgotten hour.
I want them back – ironed, crisp and new.

## Splinters

Splinters usually work their own way out,
if not they can stay embedded in soft flesh
generating their own special poison.

Like you, they can lie beneath the skin,
a tiny sliver of thorn or wood,
a throbbing black point –

So I will have to find a needle
and redden the end to a bright poker
to winkle and hook you out
painfully, slowly – but oh, the relief!

## The Betrayal

Heat bores my bones as exiled
from home I am unpicked,
stitch by careful stitch,
by your treachery. My children
ripped like paper dolls
from my side.
This blueness mocks.
Such unnecessary exotica,
velvet night inky
as a starling's wing
a widow's muslin veil.
For I too am in mourning
would grow venomous,
black bile rising in my throat,
to crunch my children's bones
and spit them on the sea-washed stones –
for you have undone me at last –
I flap useless in the wind
flat and bleached as a cotton sheet.

## New Year

The year opens its legs.
Alone I stand here
neither what I was
nor what I might become,
midwife and witness
to its re-birthing.

It does not nurture, this landscape
where winter light bends
to the curve of cloud and hillside.
The watery sun lacks conviction.

Now we enter the months of darkness,
the months of black silence,
skin flailed by wind,
cattle-prints pockmark the fields
with hoof-holes of ice.

Stiff blades of grass glisten
with rime under a vitreous moon
sheep clump like snow against
hedgerows brittle as bones.

Below the frozen mud albino roots
vulnerable, embryonic
secretly claw into metalled ground.

From a stook of dead reeds
a mallard starts, wing-tips
iridesce against the dark current
but the river flows on
silent, numb with cold
constant only to itself.

Poised between memory and desire
I receive the cold child.

## Point of Departure

So this is all it is:
after all the small despairs
those fragile little triumphs
unfolding into the promise
of a future like this train
slipping smooth as a white hand
into the gloved night.
This is the pivot, the fulcrum
the point between
somewhere and nowhere
where becoming slithers
like rain down
the window to merge into
the silvered mercury
of I have become.
Outside the wet night weeps
on Tring, on Leighton Buzzard
and Milton Keynes, on gardens
and bike sheds, on the secret lives
behind closed curtains dotted
along the Northampton line.
Ahead there is only more dark.
No horizon beckons, no cantatas
or fugues, no press of rib
or muscle of thigh. Only
the continuous timpani of rain
tattooing the roofs of taxis
and trains gushing from
the covers of overtaxed drains,
soaking, soaking me
through to the skin.

## Flatlands

A white sail cuts across
the fields angled against
a vertical of reeds.
Here where sea, land and sky
level into greyness
and a weight of cloud presses
the fens, dogs run to and fro
on invisible threads, walkers
batten down against a flurry
of rain. The wind blows
off the Russian steppes.

This is not my place.
I walk alone at the centre
of my silence. A stranger
I came to these flat lands
to drown in pools of sky,
an incandescence of shifting cloud,
to enter the deep spaces of myself.
For I have come so far.

Winter advances.
Across the marsh a tern's cry
stipples the salt wind
like the last wail of a newborn
and I am unbounded,
beneath my skin merged
with the now of grey spume,
with the call of curlew and eider,
with this prism of fractured
eastern light, this point
where loss and desire dissolve
into their own emptiness,
into this limpid opacity
and I am still.